D1243324

☆ CHEER SPIRIT ☆

QUEST

FOR THE

BEST

Conquering Cheerleading Tryouts and Competitions

by Rebecca Rissman

Consultant:
Tara L. Wieland
Owner and Head Coach
Michigan Storm Cheer and Dance
Midland, Michigan

CAPSTONE PRESS
a capstone imprint

Snap Books are published by Capstone Press,
1710 Roe Crest Drive, North Mankato, Minnesota 56003
www.capstonepub.com

Library of Congress Cataloging-in-Publication Data
Rissman, Rebecca.
  Quest for the best : conquering cheerleading tryouts and competitions / by
Rebecca Rissman.
     pages cm. -- (Cheer Spirit)
  Includes webography.
  Includes bibliographical references and index.
  Summary: "Provides practical advice for cheerleading tryouts and
competitions"—Provided by publisher.
ISBN 978-1-4914-5205-9 (library binding)
ISBN 978-1-4914-5221-9 (eBook PDF)
1. Cheerleading—Juvenile literature. 2. Cheerleading—Competitions—
Juvenile literature. I. Title.
  LB3635.R575 2016
  791.6′4—dc23
                         2015009572

Editorial Credits
Abby Colich, editor; Heidi Thompson, designer; Tracy Cummins,
media researcher; Katy LaVigne, production specialist

Photo Credits
Alamy: Evan Hurd, 25 Bottom, ZUMA Press/Jeff Cook/Quad-City Times, 11;
Capstone Press: Karon Dubke, 5, 13, 15, 19, 26, 28 Top, 28 Bottom, 29; Getty
Images: Bethany Clarke, 24; Newscom: Doug Murray/Icon, 17, St. Petersburg
Times/ZUMAPRESS.com, 18; Shutterstock: Aspen Photo, 10, bogdanhoda,
9 Top, Lilyana Vynogradova, 23, muzsy, 16, Pavel L Photo and Video, 6, 20,
25 Top, Prasit Rodphan, 9 Bottom, Robert Adrian Hillman, Design Element,
Studio64, Design Element, zsooofija, Design Element; Thinkstock: Creatas, 30,
IPGGutenbergUKLtd, Cover

Printed in the United States of America in North Mankato, Minnesota.
052015   008823CGF15

TABLE OF CONTENTS

HAVE NO FEAR! IT'S TIME TO CHEER!

Performing in front of others can be stressful. This is especially true for cheerleading tryouts and competitions. Most cheerleaders must try out to make a team or squad. During tryouts, cheerleaders usually perform in front of coaches.

Many cheerleading squads may enter competitions. In these events, cheerleaders perform choreographed routines in front of judges.

If you have an upcoming tryout or competition, you may feel unprepared or nervous. These events may cause a lot of anxiety, but they can also be fun and rewarding.

Great cheerleaders are strong and fit. They have a great attitude and are self-confident. They are also prepared. Working on these skills will help you conquer any tryout or competition.

CHEER TIP!

Choreography is the arrangement of dance or motion. Choreographers create dance or cheerleading routines.

There are many different types of cheerleading teams. Some cheerleading teams are linked to schools. These range from young children who cheer for elementary schools to college squads. Professional squads cheer for teams in the National Football League (NFL) and National Basketball Association (NBA). Cheerleaders in these squads are adults.

Schools normally have different ranks of cheer teams. The highest level is often called the varsity team. This squad is made of the most advanced cheerleaders. Other teams might have names such as junior varsity or B-squad. Some schools even have special competition squads.

Cheerleading tryouts are usually held a few months before the start of the season. For football, cheerleading tryouts may be in the summer or spring. For basketball and wrestling, tryouts may be in the fall.

There are also centers not affiliated with schools that offer different levels of cheer teams for all ages. Instead of a tryout, cheerleaders are placed on a team after a skill evaluation. Some of these teams travel to compete in other areas. These centers may also have classes that can help prepare students for school tryouts. If this interests you, have an adult help you find a location near you.

CHEER TIP!

Why try out? Many schools and programs hold tryouts so that the coaches can group cheerleaders of different ability levels together.

7

GET READY,
GET SET,
GET IN SHAPE!

Cheerleading is a tough workout. Those who want to try out need to be ready physically. Start a fitness routine at least a month in advance. This way you won't be huffing and puffing after a few minutes into your tryout.

Work on building your heart and muscle strength as well as flexibility. Try adding the following activities into your routine. Together, these will help you get into great shape.

★ Once a day run or climb stairs while singing your school song. This exercise will strengthen your heart and lungs.

★ Do 20 push-ups, 30 sit-ups, and 40 lunges (20 on each side) when you wake up each morning. These exercises will strengthen your muscles. You'll tire less quickly during your tryout. If you make the team, keep this routine going on the days you don't have practice. It will help keep you fit and strong.

★ Stretch! After you exercise, do toe touches, side bends, and half-splits. Also stretch your wrists, ankles, and neck. This will help you become more flexible. It will also help prevent injury.

CHEER TIP!

If you're not sure you are doing an exercise correctly, ask an adult for help.

SPEND TIME UPSIDE DOWN

Some cheerleading squads may require tumbling experience. Tumbling includes cartwheels, roundoffs, and other gymnastics moves. Gymnastics classes can help you learn these skills. But do not attempt gymnastics or tumbling without formal training. This could be dangerous and lead to injury. If you want to learn these skills, ask a parent about signing up for a gymnastics class.

Another great way to prepare for tryouts is to attend a cheer camp. These are special summer programs that teach cheers, jumps, and stunts. Ask a parent to help you find a cheerleading camp near you. Cheer camp is also a great way to make new friends.

CHEER TIP!

Cheerleading is a positive and social sport. After all, cheerleaders literally lift each other up! Remember to be supportive of other cheerleaders, especially during tryouts.

WHAT TO EXPECT AT TRYOUTS

Tryouts can take a few hours, or they can take all day. Some cheerleading tryouts can even last multiple days. If you have a tryout coming up, find out ahead of time how long the tryout will be. Also find out what you are expected to wear. You also need to know if you need to bring any paperwork or get a checkup from your doctor. Learning what to expect before tryouts start will make you feel less anxious. It can also help you focus your energy on doing your best.

New Skills

The first stage of cheerleading tryouts usually involves learning a new cheer, chant, or both. This is so coaches can see how each cheerleader learns new things.

Practice!

The second stage of cheerleading tryouts is practice time. This might happen all together or in smaller groups. This is your chance to make sure you know exactly what to do. Ask questions if you aren't sure about something.

Paperwork

Most schools will need some paperwork to be completed before tryouts. This will include information about you, as well as the name and phone number of an emergency contact. An emergency contact is someone who will be called if you are injured or need immediate help. You may also have to show proof that you have had a recent physical. During a physical, a doctor makes sure you are healthy enough to participate in a sport.

SHOWTIME!

The last stage of tryouts either happens right away, or a day or two later. Cheer candidates will perform their new skills in a small group in front of the coaches or judges. They might be asked to do a routine once or multiple times. Sometimes cheerleaders might be called back to perform again in another small group. This is their chance to show the coaches how well they learn new cheers and how much spirit they can show.

WHEN WILL YOU FIND OUT?

Some schools or programs will let candidates know right away what cheerleading team they will be on. Others might take a few hours or even a few days. If this happens to you, try not to get too stressed while you're waiting to find out. Take a walk, watch a movie, or listen to some calming music.

WHAT IF YOU DON'T MAKE THE SQUAD?

Not everyone will make the cheerleading squad. If you try out and don't make the squad you wanted, keep your chin up. You may have been chosen for another squad. Or you may want to think about trying a different sport altogether. Whatever you decide, don't give up. You can always try out again next year.

CHEER TIP!

You may be asked to show tumbling skills during tryouts. Only do these if you know how. It's OK to tell the judges that you don't know how to do something if you know you can't do it safely.

PUT THOSE CHEERS TO THE TEST!

Cheerleading competitions are great places for a squad to show off its hard work. These competitions are also great for watching other squads and learning new moves. If you're headed to a cheerleading competition, you may even make some new friends. Competitions usually host cheerleading squads from around a state, region, or country.

Some competitions are small. These may feature just one round of performances. Others are very large. Competitors perform several times over two or more days. In these large competitions, teams are eliminated in each round. The winner is named after the final round.

Many cheerleading competitions also give one special squad a spirit award. This prize goes to the team that shows the most school spirit and positive attitude. Earning a spirit award is a great feat.

PRACTICE MAKES PERFECT

Before entering a cheerleading competition, a squad must learn a routine. Cheerleading routines often combine dance and cheer. Coaches may come up with a routine alone. Or they may work with a professional choreographer.

After the squad learns the routine, it's time to get down to work. The best way to prepare for a competition is to practice, practice, and practice some more! In addition to team practices, practice at home. Ask an adult to help you download the music for your team's routine. Listen to it while getting ready for school in the morning. The more familiar it seems, the more comfortable you'll feel with it.

BE PREPARED

Being prepared means more than just knowing the routine by heart. Cheerleaders have to be ready for anything. If you're heading to a competition, pack extra hair accessories, undergarments, and makeup. Remind your coach to bring a backup copy of the music. Know what time you're supposed to meet your squad. Plan to get there 10 minutes early.

A DAY AT A CHEERLEADING COMPETITION

Cheerleading competitions can be long, tiring, and stressful. Or they can be fun! Planning ahead helps a cheerleader have more fun and stress less. This sample schedule will give you an idea of what a day at a competition is like.

Sample Cheer Competition Schedule

The night before: Double check to make sure everything you need for the morning is laid out and packed. Be sure to get to bed on time so you are well rested for the next day.

7:00 a.m. Wake up early and eat a healthy breakfast.

8:00 a.m. Meet squad at school parking lot. Get on bus to ride to competition.

9:00 a.m. Arrive at competition. Get wristbands and put bags in dressing room or designated area. Finish hair and makeup.

9:30 a.m.–noon Watch other teams and cheer for everyone!

12:15–12:45 p.m. Break for lunch.

1:00 p.m. Warm up.

1:50 p.m. Showtime!

2:15–4:00 p.m. Watch other teams.

4:00–5:00 p.m. Break for judging and dinner.

5:30 p.m. Attend awards ceremony.

6:00 p.m. Take bus back to school.

TELL YOUR FRIENDS

Friendly faces in the crowd are great motivation to do your best. Give a copy of the competition schedule to your friends and family. This way they can be there to root for you from the front row!

WHAT'S THE SCORE?

Cheerleaders spend most of their time rooting for other athletes to score. Competitions are their chance to rack up the points for themselves! Points are awarded for many different parts of a routine. Judges look at these areas when scoring:

- ⭐ stunts
- ⭐ jumps
- ⭐ choreography
- ⭐ cheers
- ⭐ tumbling
- ⭐ formation
- ⭐ synchronicity
- ⭐ team spirit

The points a squad earns are added together. During a competition, cheerleaders will only see the final scores from the judges. However, many judges will release their scorecards to each squad's coach afterward. A scorecard will show how the squad scored in each category.

WHO'S JUDGING YOU?

Judges at cheerleading competitions usually have a great deal of experience in cheerleading. Some judges are professional cheerleaders or former coaches. Or they might be coaches from other districts. Choreographers may also judge cheerleading competitions.

PROFESSIONAL COMPETITIONS

Cheerleading is a sport for people of all ages, from tiny tots to adult squads. Some teams reach outstanding heights with fantastic skill. The top levels of cheerleading competitions are amazing shows of acrobatics, athleticism, and enthusiasm.

These top-level cheerleading competitions aren't just for adults. In fact, some of the greatest cheerleading squads are made up of young athletes. The United States All Star Federation and ESPN host high-level competitions for young cheerleaders each year. Many of these competitions are broadcast on TV. Try watching some of these competitions. You may find them inspiring.

If you're waiting to perform, it is easy to get caught up in the thrill of competition. You may also feel overwhelmed with the pressure to do your best.

How can you stay calm when you're worrying about sticking your stunts or piling up points? It's easy. Just follow a few simple steps.

1. Find a quiet place. Tell your coach where you're going. Then find an unused hallway or go outside.

2. Take a seat. You're probably bursting with energy, so this might seem tough. Find a comfortable seated position and close your eyes. Let your hands rest easily in your lap. Roll your head from side to side. This will relax the muscles in your neck. Relax your jaw and the muscles in your low back.

3. Breathe. Sounds simple, right? You might be surprised that this can be a bit tricky. Take long, deep, slow breaths. Focus on the sound of your breath. Use it to drown out any thoughts or worries clouding your brain. Sit still breathing deeply for 5 to 10 minutes. This little break can be just what your body and brain need to recharge before you perform!

FOOD FOR FRIENDS

Tryouts and competitions can be stressful, tense, and even scary—unless you make them fun. A great way to enjoy a day of cheerleading is to make new friends. Start a conversation by sharing a healthy, delicious snack.

Friendly Fruit Mix

Bring this delicious snack mix in a large plastic bag. Invite people to enjoy a handful.

- 1 cup dried cranberries
- ½ cup yogurt covered raisins
- ½ cup dried coconut flakes
- ½ cup chocolate chips
- ½ cup roasted peanuts

Mix and Match Cracker Snacks

This simple, protein-packed, assemble-your-own snack is always a crowd pleaser. Try different combinations of crackers, cheese, and toppings.

- 1 sleeve of whole wheat crackers
- 1 sleeve of quinoa crackers
- 2 oz. sliced low-fat cheddar cheese
- 2 oz. sliced low-fat Swiss cheese
- 2 oz. sliced low-fat pepper jack cheese
- 6 oz. hummus

Packing List

Competition day is this weekend, and you've got a lot on your mind! How can you be sure you won't forget anything? Be extra prepared and make a packing list one or two days in advance.

Here's a sample packing list. What other items would you add?

★ **cheerleading uniform**
  - ★ cheerleading skirt
  - ★ cheerleading bloomers
  - ★ cheerleading top
  - ★ socks
  - ★ cheerleading shoes
  - ★ hair bow

★ **drink and snacks**
  - ★ bottle of water
  - ★ trail mix

★ **cosmetics supplies**
  - ★ brush
  - ★ hairspray
  - ★ makeup

★ **extras**
  - ★ comfortable clothes to wear before and after your performance
  - ★ music player to listen to on the bus

READ MORE

Hunt, Sara R. *You've Got Spirit! Cheers, Chants, Tips, and Tricks Every Cheerleader Needs to Know*. Minneapolis: Millbrook Press, 2013.

Webb, Margaret. *Pump It Up Cheerleading*. Sports Starters. New York: Crabtree Publishing, 2012.

Webber, Rebecca. *Varsity's Ultimate Guide to Cheerleading*. New York: Little, Brown, and Company, 2014.

Welsh, Piper. *Cheerleading*. Fun Sports for Fitness. Vero Beach, Fla.: Rourke Educational Media, 2013.

INTERNET SITES

FactHound offers a safe, fun way to find Internet sites related to this book. All of the sites on FactHound have been researched by our staff.
Here's all you do:
Visit *www.facthound.com*
Type in this code: 9781491452059

Check out projects, games and lots more at
www.capstonekids.com

INDEX